A+
books

WORLD OF COLORS

China in Colors

by Marla Gamze-Pendergrast

Consultant: Hanchao Lu
Professor and Director of Graduate Studies
School of History, Technology, & Society
Georgia Institute of Technology
Atlanta, Georgia

Capstone
press

Mankato, Minnesota

Dragon dancers in red costumes perform during the Chinese New Year. The colorful dragon brings good luck. The New Year is a popular celebration in China.

Black and **white** pandas live in the mountains of southwestern China. Bamboo is the only food they eat. Pandas eat about 30 pounds (14 kilograms) of bamboo each day.

Green rice paddies dot the Chinese countryside. Rice needs a lot of water to grow. Farmers flood the paddies with water. Little dirt walls hold in the water.

White rice and noodles are served with almost every meal in China. People use chop sticks to eat their food. Many people also drink tea with their meals.

Bright **blue** sky peeks through this modern Chinese apartment building. Apartments and homes in cities are small. Country homes are bigger. Grandparents, parents, and children often live in the same home.

Gray and **brown** stones create the Great Wall of China. It twists through 4,000 miles (6,437 kilometers) of mountains, grasslands, and deserts. Many ancient rulers built parts of the wall to keep China safe.

A **green** bus waits to cross a crowded street in Hong Kong. About 40 percent of all Chinese people live in cities. The rest live in small towns and villages.

Blue, **red**, and **green** traditional Chinese clothing is worn during holidays. The colors have special meanings. Red stands for happiness and good luck. Blue and green stand for spring.

Rows of 8,000 **gray** soldiers and horses stand at attention. The first emperor of China created the Terra Cotta Warriors to guard his tomb. They were underground for more than 2,000 years. Farmers found the clay army while digging for water.

Shanghai rises behind people in **yellow** clothing as they practice tai chi. Shanghai is the largest city in China. Its shipping port is one of the busiest in the world.

Children in **black** uniforms study martial arts. Martial arts is a form of exercise. It is sometimes used for self-defense. The Chinese have practiced martial arts for thousands of years. Chinese children also enjoy basketball and soccer.

The Yangtze River flows past China's **green** hillsides. It is the longest river in China. Many people work and live along its shores.

White stone steps lead to the **red** and **gold** Forbidden City in Beijing. It was home to many of China's past emperors and their families. Today, it is a museum where visitors can learn about China's rich history.

FACTS about China

Capital City: Beijing

Population: 1,321,851,888

Official Language: Mandarin

Common Phrases

English	Mandarin	Pronunciation
hello	ni hao	(NEE HOW)
good-bye	zài jiàn	(ZEYE JEE-en)
yes	shì de	(SHEE DEE)
no	bú shì	(BOO SHEE)

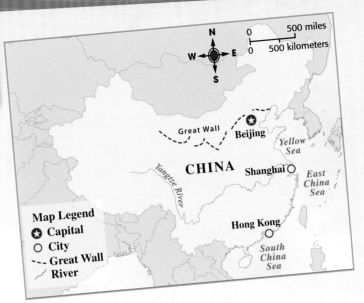

Map Legend
- ★ Capital
- ○ City
- - - - Great Wall
- ⌇ River

Great Wall

★ Beijing

Yellow Sea

CHINA

Shanghai ○

East China Sea

Hong Kong ○

South China Sea

Yangtze River

N
W E
S

0   500 miles
0   500 kilometers

Flag

Money

Chinese money
is called Renminbi.
One yuan equals
ten jiao.

jiao

yuan

Glossary

ancient (AYN-shunt) — from a long time ago

bamboo (bam-BOO) — a tropical grass with a hard, hollow stem

celebration (sel-uh-BRAY-shuhn) — a special gathering

emperor (EM-puhr-uhr) — a male ruler of a country or group of countries

grassland (GRASS-land) — a large, open area where grass and low plants grow

modern (MOD-urn) — up-to-date or new in style

paddy (PAD-ee) — a wet field where rice is grown

tai chi (TY CHEE) — an ancient form of Chinese exercise and movement

tomb (TOOM) — a grave, room, or building used for holding a dead body

traditional (truh-DISH-uhn-uhl) — passed down through time

Read More

Olson, Nathan. *China: A Question and Answer Book.* Questions and Answers. Mankato, Minn.: Capstone Press, 2005.

Schroeder, Holly. *China ABCs: A Book about the People and Places of China.* Country ABCs. Minneapolis: Picture Window Books, 2004.

Internet Sites

FactHound offers a safe, fun way to find Internet sites related to this book. All of the sites on FactHound have been researched by our staff.

Here's how:

1. Visit www.facthound.com

2. Choose your grade level.

3. Type in this book ID **1429616989** for age-appropriate sites. You may also browse subjects by clicking on letters, or by clicking on pictures and words.

4. Click on the **Fetch It** button.

FactHound will fetch the best sites for you!

Index

A+ Books are published by Capstone Press,
151 Good Counsel Drive, P.O. Box 669, Mankato, Minnesota 56002.
www.capstonepress.com

1 2 3 4 5 6 13 12 11 10 09 08

Library of Congress Cataloging-in-Publication Data
Gamze-Pendergrast, Marla.
    China in colors / by Marla Gamze-Pendergrast.
    p. cm. — (A+ books. World of colors)
    Summary: "Simple text and striking photographs present China, its culture,
and its geography" — Provided by publisher.
    Includes bibliographical references and index.
    ISBN-13: 978-1-4296-1698-0 (hardcover)
    ISBN-10: 1-4296-1698-9 (hardcover)
    1. China — Pictorial works — Juvenile literature. I. Title. II. Series.
DS712.G34 2009   2008005269
951 — dc22

Credits
Megan Peterson, editor; Veronica Bianchini, designer; Wanda Winch, photo researche

Photo Credits
AP Images/Anat Givon, 2–3; Art Life Images/age fotostock/Herve Donnezan, 14–15;
Art Life Images/age fotostock/Toño Labra, 12–13; Art Life Images/age fotostock/
Werner Otto, 10–11; Capstone Press/Karon Dubke, 8–9; Getty Images Inc./Riser/joSo
20–21; The Image Works/Justin Guariglia, 22–23; The Image Works/Lee Snider, 16–
The Image Works/Panorama, 26–27; Paul Baker, 29 (coins); Peter Arnold/Thomas
Roetting, 6–7; Shutterstock/Christophe Testi, cover; Shutterstock/Ke Wang, 1, 18–19,
Shutterstock/Luisa Fernanda Gonzalez, 29 (banknotes); Shutterstock/Regien Paassen
4–5; Shutterstock/Stephen Rudolph, 24–25; StockHaus Ltd., 29 (flag)

Note to Parents, Teachers, and Librarians
This World of Colors book uses full-color photographs and a nonfiction format
to introduce children to basic topics in the study of countries. *China in Colors*
is designed to be read aloud to a pre-reader or to be read independently by an
early reader. Photographs help listeners and early readers understand the text
and concepts discussed. The book encourages further learning by including the
following sections: Facts about China, Glossary, Read More, Internet Sites, and
Index. Early readers may need assistance using these features.